His Holiness John Paul II

cordially imparts the requested

Apostolic Blessing to

Charlotte Demi Hunt

and invokes an abundance of divine graces

Ex Aedibus Vaticanis die 17.9. 2003

+ Oscar Rizzato

Archiepiscopus

Eleemosynarius Summi Pontificis

For children of all ages, of God

Margaret K. McElderry Books   An imprint of Simon & Schuster Children's Publishing Division   1230 Avenue of the Americas, New York, New York 10020   Copyright © 2005 by Demi   All rights reserved, including the right of reproduction in whole or in part in any form.   Book design by Michael Nelson   The text for this book is set in Minister.   The illustrations for this book are rendered in paint and ink.   Title calligraphy by Jeanyee Wong   Manufactured in China

2 4 6 8 10 9 7 5 3 1

LIBRARY OF CONGRESS CATALOGING-IN-PUBLICATION DATA: Bible. English. Authorized. Selections. 2005   Jesus / [compiled by] Demi—1st ed.   p. cm.   ISBN 0-689-86905-3 (ISBN-13: 978-0-689-86905-1) (hardcover)   1. Jesus Christ—Biography—Sources, Biblical—Juvenile literature. I. Demi. II. Title.   BT299.3.D46 2005   226'.052036—dc22   2004012854

THIS TEXT IS INSPIRED BY BIBLICAL PASSAGES TAKEN FROM THE KING JAMES VERSION OF THE HOLY BIBLE, PUBLISHED BY THE NATIONAL BIBLE PRESS, PHILADELPHIA, PA.

FIRST
EDITION

"For God so loved the world, that he gave his only begotten Son, that whosoever believeth in him should not perish, but have everlasting life."

JOHN 3:16

THE ASCENSION

"And, lo, I am with you alway, even unto the end of the world." Amen.

MATTHEW 28:20

So then after the Lord had spoken unto them, he was received up into heaven, and sat on the right hand of God.

MARK 16:19

JESUS APPEARS TO THE DISCIPLES

Then the eleven disciples went away into Galilee, into a mountain where Jesus had appointed them. And when they saw him, they worshipped him: but some doubted.

And Jesus came and spake unto them, saying, "All power is given unto me in heaven and in earth. Go ye therefore, and teach all nations, baptizing them in the name of the Father, and of the Son, and of the Holy Ghost: teaching them to observe all things whatsoever I have commanded you: and, lo, I am with you alway, even unto the end of the world." Amen.

MATTHEW 28:16–20

THE RESURRECTION

And, behold, there was a great earth-quake: for the angel of the Lord descended from heaven, and came and rolled back the stone from the [grave], and sat upon it. His countenance was like lightning, and his raiment white as snow: and for fear of him the keepers did shake, and became as dead men.

And the angel answered and said unto the women, "Fear not ye: for I know that ye seek Jesus, which was crucified. He is not here: for he is risen, as he said. Come, see the place where the Lord lay. And go quickly, and tell his disciples that he is risen from the dead; and, behold, he goeth before you into Galilee; there shall ye see him: lo, I have told you."

MATTHEW 28:2–7

rent; and the graves were opened; and many bodies of the saints which slept arose, and came out of the graves after his resurrection, and went into the holy city, and appeared unto many.

MATTHEW 27:51–53

THE DESCENT AND BURIAL

And after this Joseph of Arimathaea, being a disciple of Jesus, but secretly for fear of the Jews, besought Pilate that he might take away the body of Jesus: and Pilate gave him leave. He came therefore, and took the body of Jesus.

And there came also Nicodemus, which at the first came to Jesus by night, and brought a mixture of myrrh and aloes. . . . Then took they the body of Jesus, and wound it in linen clothes with the spices, as the manner of the Jews is to bury.

Now in this place where he was crucified there was a garden; and in the garden a new sepulchre, wherein was never man yet laid. There laid they Jesus therefore because of the Jews' preparation day; for the sepulchre was nigh at hand.

JOHN 19:38–42

And the women also, which came with [Jesus] from Galilee, followed after, and beheld the sepulchre, and how his body was laid.

LUKE 23:55

THE CRUCIFIXION

Then released he Barabbas unto them: and when he had scourged Jesus, he delivered him to be crucified.

MATTHEW 27:26

Then said Jesus, "Father, forgive them; for they know not what they do."

LUKE 23:34

And about the ninth hour Jesus cried with a loud voice, saying, "Eli, Eli, lama sabachthani?" that is to say, My God, my God, why hast thou forsaken me?

MATTHEW 27:46

And there was a darkness over all the earth. . . . And the sun was darkened. . . . And when Jesus had cried with a loud voice, he said, "Father, into thy hands I commend my spirit:" and having said thus, he gave up the ghost.

LUKE 23:44–46

And when the centurion, which stood over against [Jesus], saw that he so cried out, and gave up the ghost, he said, "Truly this man was the Son of God."

MARK 15:39

And, behold, the vail of the temple was rent in twain from the top to the bottom; and the earth did quake, and the rocks

ECCE HOMO • BEHOLD THE MAN

Now at that feast [Pilate] released unto them one prisoner, whomsoever they desired. And there was one named Barabbas, which lay bound with them that had made insurrection with him, who had committed murder in the insurrection. And the multitude crying aloud began to desire him to do as he had ever done unto them.

But Pilate answered them, saying, "Will ye that I release unto you the King of the Jews?" For he knew that the chief priests had delivered him for envy.

But the chief priests moved the people, that he should rather release Barabbas unto them.

And Pilate answered and said again unto them, "What will ye then that I shall do unto him whom ye call the King of the Jews?"

And they cried out again, "Crucify him."

MARK 15:6–13

THE TRIAL OF JESUS

When the morning was come, all the chief priests and elders of the people took counsel against Jesus to put him to death: And when they had bound him, they led him away, and delivered him to Pontius Pilate the governor. . . .

And Jesus stood before the governor: and the governor asked him, saying, "Art thou the King of the Jews?" And Jesus said unto him, "Thou sayest."

And when he was accused of the chief priests and elders, he answered nothing. Then said Pilate unto him, "Hearest thou not how many things they witness against thee?"

And he answered him to never a word; insomuch that the governor marvelled greatly.

MATTHEW 27:1–2, 11–14

THE ARREST OF JESUS

And while he yet spake, lo, Judas, one of the twelve, came, and with him a great multitude with swords and staves, from the chief priests and elders of the people. Now he that betrayed [Jesus] gave them a sign, saying, "Whomsoever I shall kiss, that same is he: hold him fast."

And forthwith he came to Jesus, and said, "Hail, master;" and kissed him. And Jesus said unto him, "Friend, wherefore art thou come?" Then came they, and laid hands on Jesus, and took him. . . .

In that same hour said Jesus to the multitudes, "Are ye come out as against a thief with swords and staves for to take me? I sat daily with you teaching in the temple, and ye laid no hold on me. But all this was done, that the scriptures of the prophets might be fulfilled."

Then all the disciples forsook him, and fled.

MATTHEW 26:47–50, 55–56

The Agony in the Garden of Gethsemane

Then cometh Jesus . . . unto a place called Gethsemane, and saith unto the disciples, "Sit ye here, while I go and pray yonder."

And he took with him Peter and the two sons of Zebedee, and . . . saith he unto them, "My soul is exceeding sorrowful, even unto death: tarry ye here, and watch with me." And he went a little farther, and fell on his face, and prayed, saying, "O my Father, if it be possible, let this cup pass from me: nevertheless not as I will, but as thou wilt."

And he cometh unto the disciples, and findeth them asleep, and saith unto Peter, "What, could ye not watch with me one hour? Watch and pray, that ye enter not into temptation: the spirit indeed is willing, but the flesh is weak."

He went away again the second time, and prayed, saying, "O my Father, if this cup may not pass away from me, except I drink it, thy will be done."

And he came and found them asleep again. . . . And he left them, and went away again, and prayed the third time, saying the same words. Then cometh he to his disciples, and saith unto them, "Sleep on now, and take your rest: behold, the hour is at hand, and the Son of man is betrayed into the hands of sinners. Rise, let us be going: behold, he is at hand that doth betray me."

MATTHEW 26:36–46

THE LAST SUPPER

[On] the first day of the feast of unleavened bread the disciples came to Jesus. . . . And he said, "Go into the city to such a man, and say unto him, The Master saith, My time is at hand; I will keep the passover at thy house with my disciples."

MATTHEW 26:17–18

And when the hour was come, he sat down, and the twelve apostles with him. And he said unto them, "With desire I have desired to eat this passover with you before I suffer: For I say unto you, I will not any more eat thereof, until it be fulfilled in the kingdom of God."

And he took the cup, and gave thanks, and said, "Take this, and divide it among yourselves: For I say unto you, I will not drink of the fruit of the vine, until the kingdom of God shall come."

And he took bread, and gave thanks, and brake it, and gave unto them, saying, "This is my body which is given for you: this do in remembrance of me."

Likewise also the cup after supper, saying, "This cup is the new testament in my blood, which is shed for you. But, behold, the hand of him that betrayeth me is with me on the table. And truly the Son of man goeth, as it was determined: but woe unto that man by whom he is betrayed!"

LUKE 22:14–22

Jesus Washes the Disciples' Feet

And supper being ended . . . [Jesus] poureth water into a [basin], and began to wash the disciples' feet, and to wipe them with the towel wherewith he was girded. Then cometh he to Simon Peter: and Peter saith unto him, "Lord, dost thou wash my feet?"

Jesus answered and said unto him, "What I do thou knowest not now; but thou shalt know hereafter."

Peter saith unto him, "Thou shalt never wash my feet." Jesus answered him, "If I wash thee not, thou hast no part with me. . . ."

So after he . . . was set down again, he said unto them, "Know ye what I have done to you? Ye call me Master and Lord: and ye say well; for so I am. If I then, your Lord and Master, have washed your feet; ye also ought to wash one another's feet. For I have given you an example, that ye should do as I have done to you. . . .

Verily, verily, I say unto you, that one of you shall betray me. . . . He it is, to whom I shall give a sop, when I have dipped it." And when he had dipped the sop, he gave it to Judas Iscariot. . . . Then said Jesus unto him, "That thou doest, do quickly."

He then having received the sop went immediately out: and it was night. Therefore, when he was gone out, Jesus said, "Now is the Son of man glorified, and God is glorified in him."

JOHN 13:2, 5–8, 12–15, 21, 26–27, 30–31

If any man serve me, let him follow me; and where I am, there shall also my servant be: if any man serve me, him will my Father honour.

Now is my soul troubled; and what shall I say? Father, save me from this hour: but for this cause came I unto this hour. Father, glorify thy name."

Then came there a voice from heaven, saying, "I have both glorified it, and will glorify it again." The people therefore, that stood by, and heard it, said that it thundered: others said, "An angel spake to him."

Jesus answered and said, "This voice came not because of me, but for your sakes. Now is the judgment of this world: now shall the prince of this world be cast out. And I, if I be lifted up from the earth, will draw all men unto me." This he said, signifying what death he should die.

The people answered him, "We have heard out of the law that Christ abideth forever: and how sayest thou, the Son of man must be lifted up? Who is this Son of man?"

Then Jesus said unto them, "Yet a little while is the light with you. Walk while ye have the light, lest darkness come upon you: for he that walketh in darkness knoweth not whither he goeth. While ye have light, believe in the light, that ye may be the children of light."

JOHN 12:23–36

THE ENTRY INTO JERUSALEM

On the next day much people that were come to the feast, when they heard that Jesus was coming to Jerusalem, took branches of palm trees, and went forth to meet him, and cried, "Hosanna: Blessed is the King of Israel that cometh in the name of the Lord."

And Jesus, when he had found a young ass, sat thereon; as it is written, "Fear not, daughter of Sion; behold, thy King cometh, sitting on an ass's colt."

These things understood not his disciples at the first: but when Jesus was glorified, then remembered they that these things were written of him, and that they had done these things unto him.

The people therefore that was with him when he called Lazarus out of his grave, and raised him from the dead, [bore] record. For this cause the people also met him, for that they heard that he had done this miracle.

The Pharisees therefore said among themselves, "Perceive ye how ye prevail nothing? behold, the world is gone after him." JOHN 12:12–19

THE PROPHECY

"The hour is come, that the Son of man should be glorified. Verily, verily, I say unto you, . . . He that loveth his life shall lose it; and he that hateth his life in this world shall keep it unto life eternal.

THE RAISING OF LAZARUS

Jesus . . . cometh to the grave [of Lazarus]. It was a cave, and a stone lay upon it. Jesus said, "Take ye away the stone." Martha, the sister of him that was dead, saith unto him, "Lord, by this time he stinketh: for he hath been dead four days."

Jesus saith unto her, "Said I not unto thee, that, if thou wouldest believe, thou shouldest see the glory of God?"

Then they took away the stone from the place where the dead was laid. And Jesus lifted up his eyes, and said, "Father, I thank thee that thou hast heard me. And I knew that thou hearest me always: but because of the people which stand by I said it, that they may believe that thou hast sent me." And when he thus had spoken, he cried with a loud voice, "Lazarus, come forth."

And he that was dead came forth, bound hand and foot with graveclothes: and his face was bound about with a napkin. Jesus saith unto them, "Loose him, and let him go."

Then many of the Jews which came to Mary, and had seen the things which Jesus did, believed on him. But some of them went their ways to the Pharisees, and told them what things Jesus had done.

JOHN 11:38–46

THE TRANSFIGURATION OF JESUS

Jesus taketh Peter, James, and John his brother, and bringeth them up into [a] high mountain apart, and was transfigured before them: and his face did shine as the sun, and his raiment was white as the light.

And, behold, there appeared unto them Moses and Elias talking with him. Then answered Peter, and said unto Jesus, "Lord, it is good for us to be here: if thou wilt, let us make here three tabernacles; one for thee, and one for Moses, and one for Elias."

While he yet spake, behold, a bright cloud overshadowed them: and behold a voice out of the cloud, which said, "This is my beloved Son, in whom I am well pleased; hear ye him."

And when the disciples heard it, they fell on their face, and were sore afraid. And Jesus came and touched them, and said, "Arise, and be not afraid."

And when they had lifted up their eyes, they saw no man, save Jesus only. And as they came down from the mountain, Jesus charged them, saying, "Tell the vision to no man, until the Son of man be risen again from the dead."

MATTHEW 17:1–9

THE NEW COMMANDMENT

"A new commandment I give unto you,
That ye love one another; as I have loved
you, that ye also love one another. By
this shall all men know that ye are my
disciples, if ye have love one to another."

JOHN 13:34–35

THE GOOD SHEPHERD

"I am the good shepherd: the good shepherd giveth his life for the sheep. But he that is [a] hireling, and not the shepherd, whose own the sheep are not, seeth the wolf coming, and leaveth the sheep, and fleeth: and the wolf catcheth them, and scattered the sheep.

The hireling fleeth, because he is [a] hireling, and careth not for the sheep. I am the good shepherd, and know my sheep, and am known of mine. As the Father knoweth me, even so know I the Father: and I lay down my life for the sheep."

JOHN 10:11–15

THE KINGDOM OF GOD

"So is the kingdom of God, as if a man should cast seed into the ground; and should sleep, and rise night and day, and the seed should spring and grow up, he knoweth not how. For the earth bringeth forth fruit of herself; first the blade, then the ear, after that the full corn in the ear. But when the fruit is brought forth, immediately he putteth in the sickle, because the harvest is come."

MARK 4:26–29

THE KINGDOM OF HEAVEN

"The kingdom of heaven is like to a grain of mustard seed, which a man took, and sowed in his field: Which indeed is the least of all seeds: but when it is grown, it is the greatest among herbs, and becometh a tree, so that the birds of the air come and lodge in the branches thereof."

MATTHEW 13:31–32

THE GOOD SAMARITAN

A certain lawyer . . . said unto Jesus, "And who is my neighbour?"

And Jesus answering said, "A certain man went down from Jerusalem to Jericho, and fell among thieves, which stripped him of his raiment, and wounded him, and departed, leaving him half dead. And by chance there came down a certain priest that way: and when he saw him, he passed by on the other side. And likewise a Levite, when he was at the place, came and looked on him, and passed by on the other side.

But a certain Samaritan, as he journeyed, came where he was: and when he saw him, he had compassion on him, and went to him, and bound up his wounds, pouring in oil and wine, and set him on his own beast, and brought him to an inn, and took care of him. And on the morrow when he departed, he took out two pence, and gave them to the host, and said unto him, 'Take care of him; and whatsoever thou spendest more, when I come again, I will repay thee.'

Which now of these three, thinkest thou, was neighbour unto him that fell among thieves?"

And he said, "He that shewed mercy on him." Then said Jesus unto him, "Go, and do thou likewise."

LUKE 10:25, 29–37

Become As Little Children

Came the disciples unto Jesus, saying, "Who is the greatest in the kingdom of heaven?"

And Jesus called a little child unto him, and set him in the midst of them, And said, "Verily I say unto you, Except ye be converted, and become as little children, ye shall not enter into the kingdom of heaven. Whosoever therefore shall humble himself as this little child, the same is greatest in the kingdom of heaven. And whoso shall receive one such little child in my name receiveth me. But whoso shall offend one of these little ones which believe in me, it were better for him that a millstone were hanged about his neck, and that he were drowned in the depth of the sea."

MATTHEW 18:1–6

PETER DECLARES JESUS TO BE THE CHRIST

When Jesus came into the coasts of Caesarea Philippi, he asked his disciples, saying, "Whom do men say that I the Son of man am?"

And they said, "Some say that thou art John the Baptist; some, Elias; and others, Jeremias, or one of the prophets."

He saith unto them, "But whom say ye that I am?"

And Simon Peter answered and said, "Thou art the Christ, the Son of the living God."

And Jesus answered and said unto him, "Blessed art thou, Simon Barjona: for flesh and blood hath not revealed it unto thee, but my Father which is in heaven. And I say also unto thee, That thou art Peter, and upon this rock I will build my church; and the gates of hell shall not prevail against it. And I will give unto thee the keys of the kingdom of heaven: and whatsoever thou shalt bind on earth shall be bound in heaven: and whatsoever thou shalt loose on earth shall be loosed in heaven."

MATTHEW 16:13–19

JESUS WALKS ON WATER

And straightway Jesus constrained his disciples to get into a ship, and to go before him unto the other side, while he sent the multitudes away.

And . . . he went up into a mountain to pray.

But the ship was now in the midst of the sea, tossed with waves: for the wind was contrary. And in the fourth watch of the night Jesus went unto them, walking on the sea. And when the disciples saw him walking on the sea, they were troubled, saying, "It is a spirit;" and they cried out for fear.

But straightway Jesus spake unto them, saying, "Be of good cheer; it is I; be not afraid."

And Peter answered him and said, "Lord, if it be thou, bid me come unto thee on the water."

And he said, "Come." And when Peter was come down out of the ship, he walked on the water, to go to Jesus. But when he saw the wind boisterous, he was afraid; and beginning to sink, he cried, saying, "Lord, save me."

And immediately Jesus stretched forth his hand, and caught him, and said unto him, "O thou of little faith, wherefore didst thou doubt?"

And when they were come into the ship, the wind ceased. Then they that were in the ship came and worshipped him, saying, "Of a truth thou art the Son of God."

MATTHEW 14:22–33

THE MIRACLE OF THE LOAVES AND FISHES

And Jesus went forth, and saw a great multitude, and was moved with compassion toward them, and he healed their sick. And when it was evening, his disciples came to him, saying, "This is a desert place, and the time is now past; send the multitude away, that they may go into the villages, and buy themselves victuals."

But Jesus said unto them, "They need not depart; give ye them to eat."

And they say unto him, "We have here but five loaves, and two fishes."

He said, "Bring them hither to me." And he commanded the multitude to sit down on the grass, and took the five loaves, and the two fishes, and looking up to heaven, he blessed, and brake, and gave the loaves to his disciples, and the disciples to the multitude. And they did all eat, and were filled: and they took up of the fragments that remained twelve baskets full. And they that had eaten were about five thousand men, beside women and children.

MATTHEW 14:14–21

Naming the Apostles

And when [Jesus] had called unto him his twelve disciples, he gave them power against unclean spirits, to cast them out, and to heal all manner of sickness and all manner of disease.

Now the names of the twelve apostles are these; The first, Simon, who is called Peter, and Andrew his brother; James . . . and John his brother; Philip, and Bartholomew; Thomas, and Matthew . . . ; James . . . and Lebbaeus whose surname was Thaddaeus; Simon . . . , and Judas Iscariot, who also betrayed him. . . .

Then said Jesus unto his disciples, "If any man will come after me, let him deny himself, and take up his cross, and follow me.

For whosoever will save his life shall lose it: and whosoever will lose his life for my sake shall find it.

For what is a man profited, if he shall gain the whole world, and lose his own soul? or what shall a man give in exchange for his soul?

For the Son of man shall come in the glory of his Father with his angels; and then he shall reward every man according to his works.

Verily I say unto you, There be some standing here, which shall not taste of death, till they see the Son of man coming in his kingdom."

MATTHEW 10:1–4; 16:24–28

Blessed are they which do hunger and thirst after righteousness: for they shall be filled.

Blessed are the merciful: for they shall obtain mercy.

Blessed are the pure in heart: for they shall see God.

Blessed are the peacemakers: for they shall be called the children of God.

Blessed are they which are persecuted for righteousness' sake: for theirs is the kingdom of heaven.

Blessed are ye, when men shall revile you, and persecute you, and shall say all manner of evil against you falsely, for my sake.

Rejoice, and be exceeding glad: for great is your reward in heaven: for so persecuted they the prophets which were before you.

Ye are the salt of the earth: but if the salt have lost his savour, wherewith shall it be salted? it is thenceforth good for nothing, but to be cast out, and to be trodden under foot of men.

Ye are the light of the world. A city that is set on [a] hill cannot be hid.

Pray ye: Our Father which art in heaven, Hallowed be thy name. Thy kingdom come. Thy will be done in earth, as it is in heaven. Give us this day our daily bread. And forgive us our debts, as we forgive our debtors. And lead us not into temptation, but deliver us from evil: For thine is the kingdom, and the power, and the glory, for ever. Amen."

MATTHEW 5:1–14; 6:9–13

JESUS SUMMONS HIS FIRST DISCIPLES

Jesus began to preach, and to say, "Repent: for the kingdom of heaven is at hand."

And Jesus, walking by the sea of Galilee, saw two brethren, Simon called Peter, and Andrew his brother, casting a net into the sea: for they were fishers. And he saith unto them, "Follow me, and I will make you fishers of men." And they straightway left their nets, and followed him. . . .

And Jesus went about all Galilee, teaching in their synagogues, and preaching the gospel of the kingdom, and healing all manner of sickness and all manner of disease among the people. And his fame went throughout all Syria: and they brought unto him all sick people that were taken with divers[e] diseases and torments, and those which were possessed with devils, and those which were lunatick, and those that had the palsy; and he healed them.

And there followed him great multitudes of people.

MATTHEW 4:17–20, 23–25

THE SERMON ON THE MOUNT

And seeing the multitudes, he went up into a mountain: and when he was set, his disciples came unto him: And he opened his mouth, and taught them, saying,

"Blessed are the poor in spirit: for theirs is the kingdom of heaven.

Blessed are they that mourn: for they shall be comforted.

Blessed are the meek: for they shall inherit the earth.

thou be the Son of God, cast thyself down from hence: For it is written, He shall give his angels charge over thee, to keep thee: And in their hands they shall bear thee up, lest at any time thou dash thy foot against a stone."

And Jesus answering said unto him, "It is said, Thou shalt not tempt the Lord thy God."

And when the devil had ended all the temptation, he departed.

LUKE 4:1–13

JESUS CLEANSES THE TEMPLE

And the Jews' passover was at hand, and Jesus went up to Jerusalem, and found in the temple those that sold oxen and sheep and doves, and the changers of money sitting: And when he had made a scourge of small cords, he drove them all out of the temple, and the sheep, and the oxen; and poured out the changers' money, and overthrew the tables; And said unto them that sold doves, "Take these things hence; make not my Father's house [a] house of merchandise."

And his disciples remembered that it was written, The zeal of thine house hath eaten me up.

JOHN 2:13–17

THE TEMPTATION OF JESUS

And Jesus being full of the Holy Ghost returned from Jordan, and was led by the Spirit into the wilderness, being forty days tempted of the devil. And in those days he did eat nothing: and when they were ended, he afterward hungered. And the devil said unto him, "If thou be the Son of God, command this stone that it be made bread."

And Jesus answered him, saying, "It is written, That man shall not live by bread alone, but by every word of God."

And the devil, taking him up into [a] high mountain, shewed unto him all the kingdoms of the world in a moment of time. And the devil said unto him, "All this power will I give thee, and the glory of them: for that is delivered unto me; and to whomsoever I will I give it. If thou therefore wilt worship me, all shall be thine."

And Jesus answered and said unto him, "Get thee behind me, Satan: for it is written, Thou shalt worship the Lord thy God, and him only shalt thou serve."

And [the devil] brought him to Jerusalem, and set [Jesus] on a pinnacle of the temple, and said unto him, "If

THE MIRACLE OF CHANGING WATER INTO WINE

There was a marriage in Cana of Galilee; and the mother of Jesus was there: And both Jesus was called, and his disciples, to the marriage. And when they wanted wine, the mother of Jesus saith unto him, "They have no wine."

Jesus saith unto her, "Woman, what have I to do with thee? mine hour is not yet come."

His mother saith unto the servants, "Whatsoever he saith unto you, do it."

And there were set there six waterpots of stone. . . . Jesus saith unto them, "Fill the waterpots with water." And they filled them up to the brim. And he saith unto them, "Draw out now, and bear unto the governor of the feast." And they [bore] it.

When the ruler of the feast had tasted the water that was made wine, and knew not whence it was: (but the servants which drew the water knew;) the governor of the feast called the bridegroom, and saith unto him, "Every man at the beginning doth set forth good wine; and when men have well drunk, then that which is worse: but thou hast kept the good wine until now."

This beginning of miracles did Jesus in Cana of Galilee, and manifested forth his glory; and his disciples believed on him.

JOHN 2:1–11

THE BAPTISM OF JESUS

In those days came John the Baptist, preaching in the wilderness of Judaea, and saying, "Repent ye: for the kingdom of heaven is at hand. . . . I indeed baptize you with water unto repentance: but he that cometh after me is mightier than I, whose shoes I am not worthy to bear: he shall baptize you with the Holy Ghost, and with fire:"

Then cometh Jesus from Galilee to Jordan unto John, to be baptized of him. But John forbad him, saying, "I have need to be baptized of thee, and comest thou to me?"

And Jesus answering said unto him, "Suffer it to be so now: for thus it becometh us to fulfill all righteousness." Then he suffered him. And Jesus, when he was baptized, went up straightway out of the water: and, lo, the heavens were opened unto him, and he saw the Spirit of God descending like a dove, and lighting upon him: And lo a voice from heaven, saying, "This is my beloved Son, in whom I am well pleased."

MATTHEW 3:1–2, 11, 13–17

went up to Jerusalem after the custom of the feast. And when they had fulfilled the days, as they returned, the child Jesus tarried behind in Jerusalem; and Joseph and his mother knew not of it. But they, supposing him to have been in the company, went a day's journey; and they sought him among their kinsfolk and acquaintance. And when they found him not, they turned back again to Jerusalem, seeking him.

And it came to pass, that after three days they found him in the temple, sitting in the midst of the doctors, both hearing them, and asking them questions. And all that heard him were astonished at his understanding and answers. . . . and his mother said unto him, "Son, why hast thou thus dealt with us? behold, thy father and I have sought thee sorrowing." And he said unto them, "How is it that ye sought me? wist ye not that I must be about my Father's business?" . . .

And Jesus increased in wisdom and stature, and in favour with God and man.

LUKE 2:39–49, 52

FLIGHT INTO EGYPT

The angel of the Lord appeared to Joseph in a dream, saying, "Arise, and take the young child and his mother, and flee into Egypt, and be thou there until I bring thee word: for Herod will seek the young child to destroy him."

When he arose, he took the young child and his mother by night, and departed into Egypt: And was there until the death of Herod: that it might be fulfilled which was spoken of the Lord by the prophet, saying, "Out of Egypt have I called my son."

MATTHEW 2:13–15

JESUS CHRIST IN THE TEMPLE

And when they had performed all things according to the law of the Lord, they returned into Galilee, to their own city Nazareth.

And the child grew, and waxed strong in spirit, filled with wisdom: and the grace of God was upon him.

Now his parents went to Jerusalem every year at the feast of the passover. And when he was twelve years old, they

THE NATIVITY

And it came to pass in those days, that there went out a decree from Caesar Augustus, that all the world should be taxed. . . . And all went to be taxed, every one into his own city. And Joseph also went up from Galilee . . . unto the city of David, which is called Bethlehem; (because he was of the house and lineage of David:) To be taxed with Mary his espoused wife, being great with child.

And so it was, that, while they were there, the days were accomplished that she should be delivered. And she brought forth her first-born son, and wrapped him in swaddling clothes, and laid him in a manger; because there was no room for them in the inn.

LUKE 2:1, 3–7

THE ANNUNCIATION

The angel Gabriel was sent from God unto a city of Galilee, named Nazareth, to a virgin espoused to a man whose name was Joseph, of the house of David; and the virgin's name was Mary.

And the angel came in unto her, and said, "Hail, thou that art highly favoured, the Lord is with thee: blessed art thou among women. . . . Fear not, Mary: for thou hast found favour with God. And, behold, thou shalt . . . bring forth a son, and shalt call his name JESUS.

"He shall be great, and shall be called the Son of the Highest . . . and of his kingdom there shall be no end."

LUKE 1:26–28, 30–33

For unto us a child is born, unto us a
son is given: and the government shall
be upon his shoulder: and his name
shall be called Wonderful, Counsellor,
The mighty God, The everlasting
Father, The Prince of Peace.

ISAIAH 9:6

IN THE BEGINNING

was the Word, and the Word was with
God, and the Word was God. . . . All
things were made by him; and without
him was not any thing made that was
made. In him was life; and the life was
the light of men.

JOHN 1:1, 3, 4

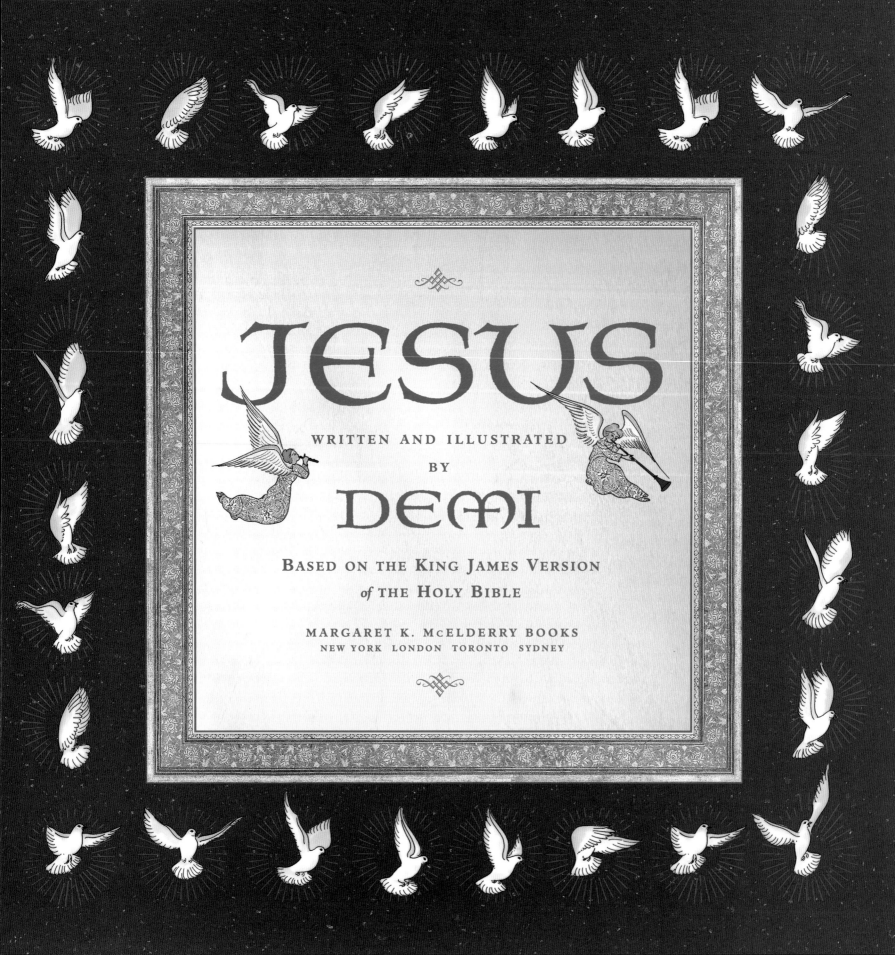

JESUS

WRITTEN AND ILLUSTRATED

BY

DEMI

BASED ON THE KING JAMES VERSION
of THE HOLY BIBLE

MARGARET K. McELDERRY BOOKS
NEW YORK LONDON TORONTO SYDNEY